The Ultimate Management Guide!

Management

Increase Your Confidence And Communication Skills, Use Creativity To Motivate And Inspire Workplace Morale, And Skyrocket Productivity!

Ryan Cooper

STOP!!! Before you read any further....Would you like to know the Secrets of Transforming your life, overcome insecurities, develop leadership skills, and undeniable confidence in your personal, professional, and relationship life?

If your answer is yes, then you are not alone. Thousands of people are looking for the secret to have unstoppable confidence and self-driven power in all areas of their lives.

If you have been searching for these answers without much luck, you're in the right place!

Not only will you gain incredible insight in this book, but because I want to make sure to give you as much value as possible, right now for a limited time you can get full **100% FREE access to a VIP bonus EBook** entitled **LIMITLESS ENERGY!**

Just Go Here For Free Instant Access:

www.PotentialRise.com

Legal Notice

Disclaimer Notice

Table Of Contents

Engagement, Motivation, Production, And Workplace Morale!"

Free Bonus Offer

Introduction

I want to thank you and congratulate you for purchasing the book, *"Management: The Ultimate Management Guide! - Increase Your Confidence And Communication Skills, Use Creativity To Motivate And Inspire Workplace Morale, And Skyrocket Productivity!"*.

Management Strategies and Techniques for Unstoppable Success!

This "Management" book contains proven steps and strategies on how to quickly and efficiently build your management abilities and confidence so you are able to build rapport, increase workplace morale, inspire and motivate with creativity, handle difficult people and situations, skyrocket productivity, and much more!

Today's modern workplaces demand more than just simple technical know-how. More than anything, the ability to deal with different sorts of people and the capacity to be bold, creative, and wise in forging long-term solutions to problems come as requisite traits for managers worth their salt.

As such, the succeeding chapters provide a detailed exploration of what you need to do if you ever aspire to be a good leader yourself. It's a worthwhile introduction to the dynamics of the workplace and the vibrancy required for any management team to keep up.

Thanks again for purchasing this book, I hope you enjoy it!

Chapter 1 - Examples Of Some Of The World's Best Managers And Their Management Styles

Writers are often told that in order to be good at what they do, they need to be voracious readers first. Why? Because reading others' works provides them the perfect opportunity to define their own tastes and style in writing.

The same is true in management. If you strive to be a good manager, you need to understand and learn from the stories of other managers who have had remarkable management career themselves. This knowledge will guide you in picking up best practices and in making you inspired enough to carve your own unique story.

Below are a few managers who have made a name for themselves, not only for their adeptness in leading their respective organizations to success, but also because of their management styles.

- **Larry Page, Google**

Lawrence "Larry" Page is the current CEO of tech giant Google. Alongside Sergey Brin, he cofounded what is now without a doubt the most successful search engine on the planet.

Today, Google is one of the world's most successful technology firms. It is a behemoth multibillion enterprise with products and services that range from search engines, video streaming sites, gadgets, and web-based ads. Its flagship site, Google.com, counts as the default search engine for billions of internet users around the world.

Larry's management style used to be one where he allowed his engineers to work on their own, believing that giving them enough breathing room and space to do their thing will result in greater productivity. Recently, however, Google implemented a radical shift in management style. Today, team leaders are required to take a more direct participation in the work of their engineers. This is founded on the idea that people work better when they receive constant feedback or validation.

- ### Indra Nooyi, PepsiCo

Consistently ranked as one of the best and most-admired CEOs in the US in the past couple of years, Indra Nooyi has the unenviable challenge of leading the world's second largest food and beverage company in the face of stiff competition. And so far she has been doing well; since her rise as chief financial officer in 2000 and in her present capacity as chairperson and CEO, profits for the company have risen up to a remarkable 72 percent.

Indra's understanding of how the market operates enables her to design strategies and policies that give her company a competitive edge. In the process, her solid background in math and physics are also put to good use.

But for all her accomplishments, the journey to where she is right now hasn't been easy. Indra admits that in fulfilling her career responsibilities, she had to make a lot of sacrifices, in particular the fact that she didn't get to spend as much time seeing her kids grow as she wanted. Her devotion to her goals is one for the books.

- ### Jeff Bezos, Amazon.com

Talk about online shopping and Amazon.com definitely ranks on top of the list. Amazon's dominance in electronic commerce can all be attributed to the boldness of vision of its chairman and CEO, Jeffrey Preston "Jeff" Bezos.

Founded in 1994 in Jeff's basement, Amazon was a small tech startup that initially focused on selling books online. Years later, it has grown by leaps and bounds and is now the world's preeminent online shopping destination that sells, not only books, but also every other conceivable item.

What makes Amazon special is that it is an enterprise that broke new grounds. Jeff's extraordinary vision has spawned a revolution in retail, making shopping from your couch a reality.

As a manager, Jeff is relentless in expanding his market and making his service available to as much people on the planet as possible. Today, despite the preponderance of one too many online shopping sites, Amazon remains an industry leader, thanks in large part to its founder's aggressive business acumen, devotion to innovation, and profound understanding of what the market wants.

If you aspire to be as successful as any of these managers, the first thing you need to develop is confidence in your management capability. The next chapter explains this point in greater detail.

Chapter 2 - How To Increase Confidence In Your Management Abilities And Lead Your Team To Excellence

Being a good manager is not an overnight exercise. To become the best version of yourself, you have to remain committed to your goals, be hard at work, and strong enough to live up to the positive management principles you impose upon yourself. In more ways than one, being a good manager is a lifestyle, a mindset and an attitude that you need to live by day in and day out.

- **Equip yourself with the technical know-how needed to get the job done.**

This is perhaps the most basic criteria that you should meet. If you want to be confident at what you do, you need to be adequately equipped with the knowledge and skills needed to create solutions. If you are in the IT field, for example, it should be a given that you have topnotch programming skills. If you are in the media sector, you should be acutely aware of how the media operates. The more knowledgeable you are in your field of expertise, the more convincing you come across as a leader.

- **Work on your communication skills.**

A huge part of management has something to do with building connections with people from different ranks. Communication is key in passing on ideas across different levels and in ensuring the organization remains cohesive. On a personal level, being a confident communicator means that you have full control of both your verbal and non-verbal language. Your choice of words, the way you look, and how you perceive yourself all play a part in how other people view you as a communicator.

- **Learn how to deal with stress.**

One of the things that you definitely have to deal with as a manager is the constant onslaught of stress. Whether you like it or not, stress comes as an inevitability in managerial positions. But this does not mean that you are ruined to a life of distress. Far from it. Rise above the negative effects of stress by learning basic stress management techniques.

- **Stay positive.**

Do away with self-doubts by sporting a "can do" mentality. If you don't choose to put yourself out there because you harbor doubts and can't deal with your insecurities, you are depriving yourself of the opportunity to grow and mature.

- **Never stop learning.**

Do not allow complacency to take root in your life. The best way to ensure dynamism in the way you think and see things is by always looking for ways to enrich your knowledge and skills. Surround yourself with the best people whom you can learn from. Attend conferences, symposia, and the like. You can even attend formal courses in the university.

The key is to be always curious and hungry for knowledge.

Chapter 3 - The Perfect Formula To World Class Management - When Management Is Excellent, Employees Also Perform Excellent, And Vice Versa

A huge part of either the success or failure of any organization's undertakings rests on the quality of its management team. That being said, different managers adhere to different management principles according to what suit their personalities and the type of organization that they represent.

There are, however, a couple of things that are mutually shared by excellent and world-class managers. These include the following:

- **Identify your goals and objectives and provide a clear course of action.**

Being a manager means that you are the leader of the pack. You don't stay behind and watch things happen while you remain passive. Rather, you provide a clear direction to what you want to happen. You are keenly aware of what you seek to achieve and you identify the ways that you need to employ in order to turn such a vision into immediate reality.

- **Have faith in your employees.**

Organizations do not revolve around a central personality, unless such an organization is a cult. If you want to be a world class manager, you need to delegate various tasks to different people because clearly you can't do everything on your own. Part of delegating tasks to your employees is sporting faith in their capabilities. Provide them with space and enough breathing room to do what they do best. Avoid micromanaging your employees because doing so fosters a stifling environment that is not conducive for growth.

- **Get involved.**

While it is true that you need to allow your employees to grow and excel without the need for you to breathe behind their backs, it is just as crucial for you to ensure that what they are doing is headed toward the realization of the organization's overall goals. You need to be clued in on what is happening on the ground, including both the challenges and positive developments.

- **Foster open communication.**

Creating a healthy and positive workplace environment requires communication. And as everyone knows, communication is a two-way street: you can't dominate the conversation, in the same way that you can't just leave the talking to others. There must be a constant exchange between you as manager and the people you manage. It is only by holding constant dialogue and vibrant exchange between members of an organization can you ensure sustained growth and innovation.

- **Innovate.**

Remaining static, or worse, complacent, is the least thing you want to deal with. In business, as in anything else, the flow of new and innovative ideas should be fluid. You just can't rest all your marbles in one basket. The dynamism and creativity of any organization can be best seen in its willingness to invest in something new.

- **Recognize achievements.**

Take some time out to acknowledge the hard work, effort, and ingenuity of your employees. After all, without them your vision will remain a vision. It is these people who make things happen, so it is imperative that you recognize their worth and positive contributions.

- **And finally, lead by example.**

As their manager, people look up to you as a leader. You're not expected to be a saint. However, you are expected to display your best in every endeavor that you undertake. This covers not only your technical know-how, but also your ability to deal with other people, as well as your capacity to inspire.

The next chapter discusses measures and techniques to help you boost the morale and happiness of your employees.

Chapter 4 - Management Techniques To Inspire Workplace Morale, Employee Happiness, And To Skyrocket Productivity

At the heart of any organization are its people. Without them, there wouldn't be any organization to speak of in the first place. As a manager, therefore, it is incumbent upon you to ensure that the workplace is not only a site of labor, but more importantly, a place that inspires and makes people happy.

From a management perspective, having a happy and satisfied workforce is beneficial for the organization. Countless studies have shown that people tend to be more productive when they are working under ideal conditions, i.e., a happy working environment. This is also good for their overall physical and emotional well-being. So when you have a happy, healthy, and an inspired workforce, you are in effect doing your organization a great favor.

Boosting the morale of your employees don't need to be elaborate or complex. Beyond financial incentives and material rewards, making them feel special and cared for is by far the best way to make them more motivated. How? Below are a few ways to get started:

- Celebrate personal events, such as birthdays.
- Organize events that involve the families of employees. These include "bring your kids to work" weekdays or junior internships.
- Provide incentive for jobs done well. These could either be gift certificates, discount cards, or little tokens of appreciation.
- Go out as a team every now and then. Grab drinks or maybe indulge in a karaoke fest. This is a great way to build a stronger bond among employees.

- Allow your employees to organize interest groups among themselves, such as clubs that cater to photography enthusiasts, sports nuts, bakers, or book lovers, among others.
- Free food is always a good motivator, particularly in days when your employees are rushing to finish an urgent project and they have little to no time at all to get off their desks and grab lunch.
- Look after your employees' physical well-being. Have a gym available at the workplace, provide discount cards for use at local gyms, and have healthy food choices available at the cafeteria. While you're at it, you can also organize sports fests.
- Hold professional development courses. You want your employees to be kept abreast with the developments in their fields, so bring in experts to discuss new trends and new ways of doing things. Consider this a wise investment for the organization.
- Organize charity drives. Nothing makes people feel happy and more motivated other than the knowledge that they have made a positive impact in the lives of those who need help.
- Have a feedback box. For suggestions, comments, complaints, or anything else that your employees wish to convey, make sure that there is a way for them to get heard.

In sum, laughter reduces stress, strengthens the bond among employees, and boosts productivity. A work environment that fosters happiness is one that guarantees its own success.

Chapter 5 - Using Creativity To Motivate Your Employees And Keep Things Light Hearted And Fun

In many of today's workplaces, it's almost impossible to use the words "fun" and "work" in the same sentence. Sadly, this speaks volumes of the less than ideal kind and quality of working conditions available in these places.

The fact of the matter is that now more than ever, people are looking for jobs that not just allow them to pay their bills, but also make them feel what they are doing is worth something valuable. This need is easily addressed by fostering a workplace that leaves room for employees to have fun and not feel as if they are stuck in a dead-end job until they retire.

Looking after the welfare and happiness of your employees need not be a costly affair. Here are a few suggestions to keep things in the workplace light hearted and fun:

- **Provide your employees an avenue to express themselves or display their creativity.**

Start by implementing Casual Fridays, where your employees can come in to work dressed in an attire other than the usual office wear. This will no doubt provide them greater leeway in their choice of clothes. To make things even fun, you can turn Casual Fridays into themed costume days, where everyone should come in to work wearing a costume.

- **Organize contests.**

Need a new and catchy one-liner for your ads? How about photos for your marketing collateral? Or maybe a poster for a sponsored event? Organize a contest involving everyone at work and come up with exciting prizes. It's a fun way for all the employees to exercise a little creativity and get rewarded for it.

- **Create a fun and engaging physical environment that ensures the productivity of your employees.**

Monolithic, cubicle workspaces are gradually becoming a thing of the past. In fact, many forward-looking organizations across the world are now taking pains to ensure that their workplaces are not only aesthetically pleasing, but also practical and worth taking pride in. So integrate design into your own workplace to improve productivity – the kind that employees can draw much-needed inspiration from.

But above all, learn to set the limits of what constitutes fun. When in doubt, always err on the side of safety. As such, discourage the use of profane words, crass and insensitive jokes, sexual banter, name-calling, personal insults, and other things that put the organization in a bad light.

Chapter 6 - Tips For Developing Your Communication Skills And Ability To Relate And Build Rapport With Your Employees

Getting along well with other people, whether they are your superiors or subordinates, is indubitably a trait any good manager must possess. By being able to communicate with people from all ranks, you are able to convey what needs to be done, listen to what others have to say, and formulate mutually beneficial policies.

This is precisely the reason why apart from having sufficient technical know-how, today's modern managers need to have excellent communication skills as well. In fact, in most classifieds, it's not at all surprising to see items such as "strong interpersonal skills" and "people person" as requisites in any managerial job posting.

Much of your duties as a manager requires you to talk with different people day in and day out, hence the indispensability of proper communication skills. But how do you exactly develop the confidence you need to rise above communication-related challenges?

- Be concise and direct to the point. You don't need to ramble on and on if you can express everything you need to say in one sentence.
- Watch your tone, pacing, and volume of your voice. Confident people speak clearly and in an audible volume. They also try to match the pacing of the people they speak with as an attempt at making themselves better understood.
- Be professional. Pay attention to your choice of words.
- Watch your mannerisms and gestures. It's possible that what you are saying can be taken out of context, particularly when the words you utter do not match your body language.

What you don't say also mean something. Even when you are silent, people will still try to gauge if you are trying to say anything through your nonverbal language. Slouching, for example, reflects poorly on you because such a habit is normally associated with insecure or lazy people.

So if you want to project confidence without saying anything, observe proper posture. Sit or stand up straight. At the same time, project a positive demeanor by making it a habit to smile always.

Building rapport

Part of having excellent communication skills is the ability to build rapport with other people. Rapport refers to an unspoken connection with another person brought about by mutual trust or emotional affinity. It can also be a form of appreciation of other people's thoughts and feelings.

Building rapport is important because it fosters open communication and mutual trust. It also enhances your likeability as a manager, which makes it less difficult for you to make people listen and take a look at what you have to say. When there is unity and less discord within the workplace, it follows that the overall productivity of everyone gets a boost.

Of course the traditional thinking is that managers should not develop close relationships with their subordinates. Tradition dictates that a certain distance must be kept in place to ensure respectability and to serve as a clear divide between you and the rest of your employees.

However, such a mindset only serves to restrict the otherwise productive dynamics at the workplace. This mentality is also counterproductive because it prevents you from appreciating your employees as people and not as just nameless and faceless aspect of your organization.

Here are a couple of ways to help you build rapport with your employees:

- Be approachable. Ask people how they are doing. At the same time, develop an open door policy. Let your employees know that you are always open to any suggestion or feedback.
- Start by dwelling on commonalities. Key to making enjoyable small talks is finding a common ground or a topic that both of you are familiar with. Start off with non-threatening subjects, such as the weather or how they go to work.
- Acknowledge jobs well done. Doing so makes your employees feel special and serves as a powerful motivational tool.
- Mind your body language. Look at people's eyes directly. Don't move about needlessly as if you should be somewhere else or should be doing something else.
- Don't be too personal. Be cautious from encroaching on the private lives of your employees. If they trust you enough and feel comfortable with you, they themselves would be the first to offer such information anyway.
- Don't be too serious. Have a sense of humor.

In all, communication is an integral aspect of management. When done right, it could foster a positive dynamic at the workplace and result in increased productivity, as well as improved professional relationships.

Chapter 7 - Management Team Building - How To Know Who To Hire For Your Management Team

There comes a point in your business when you need to delegate tasks to other people. During the nascent period, you try to do as much tasks as you can on your own. But as your business grows and your operations expand, the need to have your own management team becomes very important.

However, you just don't want to hire any manager; you want to have the best in your management team. Admittedly, it is hard to identify which kind of people will thrive in a given working environment. As such, it is imperative that you come up with a predefined set of criteria to help you filter the kind of managers you want in your team.

Here are a handful of things to consider when hiring managers:

- **Consider your present roster of employees before looking outside.**

Many organizations have an internal career development plan that takes care of their present pool of employees and identify which among these have the potential to perform well in a higher position. This works because anyone who gets promoted from the inside is already familiar with the existing working conditions, and thus needs little to no time at all to get acculturated.

Other organizations, on the contrary, choose to employ from outside under the presumption that an outsider is bound to infuse new ideas and perspectives as opposed to someone who has long been entrenched in the system.

- **Skills, knowledge, and level of expertise are things that you shouldn't compromise on.**

Check out the applicants' academic background, technical know-how, degree of creativity, leadership skills and ability to deal with different kinds of people. These are traits that you should carefully assess before even considering if they are worth hiring.

- **Don't be afraid to disqualify applicants whom you think don't fit the bill.**

Be honest with yourself. Don't dwell on an applicant who doesn't meet the requirements you have set for the post. Move on and keep looking.

- **Gauge their experience**.

Management entails a certain sense of maturity that can only be derived by years of experience. The greater and the more diverse the experience, the better. You may need to verify with former employers, ask around, conduct character check, or maybe even check an applicant's social media visibility before making your final decision.

- **Look for team players.**

It's hard to tell in one meeting if an applicant is going to perform well in your team. Looks can be deceiving, and sometimes first impressions can fail, too. The key is to identify traits that you think would be critical in the operations that this future manager would have to deal with. Look at your present organizational setup vis-à-vis the skill set and personality of the applicant, and decide if they are a good match.

Being a team player ensures that everyone is given a chance to shine and be heard. After all, a manager is supposed to bring out the best in people, not act like a dictator.

- **Trust your instincts.**

An important thing to consider in hiring managers is that they should be the sort of people whom you can trust and work with under minimal supervision. Technical skills should be a given. So do take the time out to see whether an applicant shares the same goals and vision and if he is up to the challenge of turning these into reality.

Hiring the best managers is often just the first step in building an awesome management team. The real challenge happens when these managers are put to the test, such as when they are confronted by difficult situations or unhappy customers. On this end, the next chapter discusses ways on how to better deal with angry clients.

Chapter 8 - How To Deal With Unhappy Clients And Customers And Other Difficult People

In an ideal business environment, there aren't any difficult customers. Everything is fine and dandy, and business operations are not marred by any potentially disruptive occurrence. But alas, such a setting is wishful thinking at best. As any manager will tell you, running a business is anything but a walk in the park.

One of the so-called hazards of business has something to do with the inevitability of difficult customers or clients. To a certain extent, having to deal with these sort of people comes as a given. Needless to say, it is requisite for every manager worth his or her salt to have the skills and emotional capacity to handle situations involving difficult clients.

Wisdom, ample amount of negotiation skills, ability to determine the root cause of the problem and devise feasible solutions, as well as the ability to keep your composure and work well under pressure are all integral in dealing with difficult customers.

Here are a number of pointers to get you started:

- **Do not let negative feelings or emotions get the better of you.**

Interactions with difficult customers can sometimes turn nasty, especially when they are not handled well. As a manager, the least thing you want to do is to get involved in a messy disagreement with any of your customers.

Of course as a human being with emotions, it is difficult not to get caught up with the negative vibe in situations like this. However, it takes control, maturity, and a fair amount of wisdom to keep yourself from stooping to the irate customer's level. Keeping yourself level-headed is definitely a harder choice than allowing yourself to lose your cool, but whoever said doing the right thing is easy? Stay calm and be on top of the situation from start to finish.

- **Acknowledge the client's concerns by listening.**

Sometimes all an angry customer needs is for someone to hear his or her disappointment. As such, allow the client to vent. Do not engage in a shouting match because doing so only aggravates the already difficult situation. Most angry customers are considerably easier to handle once their concern has been heard and duly acknowledged.

- **Show empathy.**

Neither you nor the customer wants to be entangled in any sort of disagreement. Who does, right? A quick and easy way to defuse the tension is by using carefully worded phrasings to let your client know that you understand what the issue is and that you are willing to go out of your way to settle it once and for all.

- **Do not be afraid to admit mistakes if there was really one.**

Covering up for a mistake isn't something that should be done at all. When the customer is indeed on the receiving end of an unjust policy or questionable transaction, do not let the whole thing drag any further. Instead, make a sincere apology and take quick concrete measures to rectify the situation.

- **Never make a promise you can't keep.**

To pacify an angry customer or as a way to escape out of a difficult spot, many managers commit the common pitfall of making promises that they themselves cannot guarantee with absolute certainty. In this scenario, the manager yields to what the customer demands as an attempt at fleeing from a sticky situation.

But this tactic is counterproductive because it does nothing to resolve the original issue. Rather, it sets the stage for another problem in the future, particularly when the promise given to the affected client turns out to be a dud.

The rule of thumb is to never make promises you can't keep. But if you need to display a show of commitment, then advise your customer the only thing you can guarantee is that you will do everything within your power and authority to get to the bottom of the case and come up with a viable solution.

At the end of the day, remember that each customer presents unique opportunities to improve how things are run within your organization. One difficult scenario is entirely different from others, so try to learn as much as you can from each situation. Avoid mistakes from ever happening again. Most importantly, be proactive in instituting reforms for areas of opportunities.

Chapter 9 - Time Management Tips For Keeping You And Your Workforce Moving Towards Excellence

Key to ensuring success in the workplace, or in any place for that matter, is effective time management. When you have a keen awareness of the value of time in relation to the goals that you and your organization have set out to accomplish, then you will be likelier than not to be prudent with its use.

Note, however, that the ability to take full control of your time does not mean that you have to create a rigid and inflexible robot-like environment. Nor does it mean that you have to inundate yourself with a seeming endless pile of tasks for much of your waking hours. Far from it.

Instead, managing your time well ensures that you, your workforce, and the entire organization are able to operate with efficiency and speed, with enough time to spare to enable you to appreciate your hard work and effort and seek personal growth outside of the workplace.

There are many advantages to subscribing to efficient time management techniques. Among these include increased productivity, a boost in efficiency, and a reduction in the stress level at the workplace.

The following are tips to help you and your workforce move towards excellence through time management:

- **Organize goals in the workplace.**

Key to successful time management is having clear knowledge of the things that you need to do and accomplish within the day or within a specific period of time. When you have a ready lineup of tasks, there's no need to guess which tasks should come first and which should come next.

The goals or tasks that you need to do should be organized according to a defined set of criteria. The most obvious way to go about your tasks is to arrange them according to urgency. But these can also be arranged according to the time needed or amount of resources needed to complete them.

- **Create a calendar.**

Many organizations normally create their own calendar of events and deadlines at the turn of each year. This way, they are able to adequately plan beforehand to avoid having to rush as the deadline looms.

- **Set deadlines and strictly adhere to them.**

Deadlines are very important in ensuring that you follow your calendar. Without deadlines, you are basically making it easy for yourself and your workforce to take a less proactive approach in your operations. A good manager should treat deadlines as sacred dates.

- **Focus on one task at a time as opposed to multitasking.**

For a long time, many people see multitasking as a better way to get done with things faster and more efficiently. Recent studies suggest, however, that doing multiple tasks at one time reduces your sense of focus and makes you prone to committing errors. As a result, you end up completing your tasks in far more time than expected.

Experts say it is better to focus on one task at a time. Doing so enables you to pay all your attention on one and only one task, helping you get done with it faster as opposed to if you were doing many other tasks at the same time.

- **Do related tasks all at once to avoid jumping from one unrelated task to another.**

If you have to reply to your emails, do so in one sitting. Avoid replying to one email then creating an Excel report then replying to another email then doing the minutes in a meeting. As much as possible, do related tasks all at once so that you do not lose your momentum and you avoid wasting time needlessly.

- **Stay clear from any sort of distraction.**

The key is to stay focused on the task at hand. Be proactive in clearing your working environment from anything that might take your attention away from what you are doing. For example, constantly checking your phone, email, or web pages will cause you to lose your focus or momentum, and in the process waste precious time. Stay clear from noise, visual clutter, or anything else that might cause you to lose your focus.

- **Learn to say no.**

Create a sense of self-awareness to identify the extent of what you are capable of accomplishing physically, mentally, and emotionally. Do not stretch yourself too thin. Otherwise, you will only end up wasting time.

- **Take a break.**

All work and no play can indeed make you dull. Learn to strike a balance between buckling down for work and taking some time out to recharge. When you keep on working for hours on end, stress can catch up on you. As indicated in the previous chapters, stress exposes you to risks of diseases and emotional volatility. It also reduces your concentration and sense of focus. When you are stressed out, you basically lose control of your time.

- **Do away with procrastination.**

Be proactive in carrying out the tasks that you are perfectly capable of completing today. This can be achieved by focusing on your goals and being disciplined enough to acknowledge that you should use your time wisely and efficiently.

Chapter 10 - Using Your Leadership Position To Build A Legacy, Set An Example, Give Back To The Community, And Care For Your Employees

The previous chapters touched on the different management techniques and strategies designed to make you an exemplary manager. But what happens once you've reached your peak?

The thing is, you don't need to reach the peak of success in order to make a difference in the lives of other people. In fact, every step you take offers an excellent opportunity to leave an impact, not only on the lives of people within your immediate environment, but also those who lie far beyond it.

So how do you leave your legacy as a manager and as a leader? Here are three ways to do so:

- **Institute policies that seek to provide long-term solutions to problems within the organization.**

Have a thorough appreciation of the issues within the workplace and commit yourself to making it a better place. Take some time out to listen to the feedback of others, then devise concrete measures to address such concerns.

For example, if people in a factory complain of perennial backaches because of standing too long while on duty, you can take this as an opportunity to take a closer look at the operating procedures within the factory itself. This should be followed by real solutions, such as dividing shifts, providing yearly appointments with a chiropractor, expanding health benefits, or maybe having therapists come over to do regular back massages.

- **Go above and beyond what is mandated of you.**

As you go about doing your work as a manager, be concerned not only with how your own career is going. Instead, take a special interest as well in the welfare of the people you work with. As indicated in the previous chapter, it is incumbent upon you as a manager to draw out the best in your employees. So keep pushing them until they reach their fullest potential and be the best in their own field. Nothing is more satisfying than seeing people under your watch earn their own share of success.

- **Share to the less fortunate.**

Beyond job titles and other fleeting forms of entitlements, another way to measure success is by the lengths you will go to extend help to those who need it. Being philanthropic should go beyond mere lip service. In other words, you need to take concrete actions and deliberate steps geared toward making other people's lives better, or at least more bearable.

Giving back to the community can come in many forms. It can come as a cash donation for a charity house or a scholarship fund for bright students coming from financially challenged families. You can also devote your time teaching kids with special needs or volunteering in other worthwhile endeavors.

In sum, being a good leader means taking the time and effort to improve your skills and knowledge, and using these to optimize operations and make people within your organization productive and happy. The journey to become the best version of your self is not an easy process, but with dedication, faith in your personal capabilities, and sheer will, everything is possible.

Conclusion

Thank you again for purchasing this book on world-class management principles and techniques!

I am extremely excited to pass this information along to you, and I am so happy that you now have read and can hopefully implement these strategies going forward.

I hope this book was able to help you gain a better understanding of effective management strategies and how integral these are not only in establishing yourself as a good leader, but also in steering your employees and the organization you represent toward success.

The next step is to get started using this information and to hopefully live a fulfilling and enriching life!

Please don't be someone who just reads this information and doesn't apply it, the strategies in this book will only benefit you if you use them!

If you know of anyone else that could benefit from the information presented here please inform them of this book.

Finally, if you enjoyed this book and feel it has added value to your life in any way, please take the time to share your thoughts and post a review on Amazon. It'd be greatly appreciated!

Thank you and good luck!

Preview Of:

The Ultimate Team Building Guide!

<u>Team Building</u>

Quickly Increase Team Building And Project Management Skills For Better Employee Engagement, Motivation, Production, And Workplace Morale!

Introduction

I want to thank you and congratulate you for purchasing the book, *"Team Building: The Ultimate Team Building Guide! - Quickly Increase Team Building And Project Management Skills For Better Employee Engagement, Motivation, Production, And Workplace Morale!"*

This "Team Building" book contains proven steps and strategies on how to quickly win over the confidence of your current team and gain the respect of new members. You will learn the basics of proper team structures and all the details of how to properly motivate for the best output of the team and each individual!

You will also learn many other skills that will help you in your abilities to lead and manage this team, such as but not limited to the following:

- How to make team building sessions work for you;

- Eliminating the road blocks that can delay the progression of your team and accomplishment of its goals;

- How to build and use power rapport skills to gain confidence and respect;

- Identifying the core elements in forming the right team building structure;

- The best steps to assign leadership and management roles within your team;

- How to develop and use your leadership charisma to build the motivation of your team and to direct team members towards the accomplishment of goals;

- How to deal with difficult or mean team members, instill discipline, improve their attitude so they become productive members like the rest;

- Proven ways on how to boost team productivity and morale;

- How to develop a culture of excellence and collaboration through enhanced leadership skills;

- You will also find creative tips to increase engagement as well as boost and sustain motivation of your team members.

All these and more await you with the purchase of this book and reading its content.

Thanks again for purchasing this book, I hope you enjoy it!

Chapter 1: Understanding The Complications Of Team Building

Understand that team building is not an overnight process. You cannot just hold a team building session for you and your staff and expect it to be an instant solution for all members to work well together. It is, however, a powerful solution and a continuing process when applied correctly.

Making the Team Building Session Work for You

In this chapter, let us unlock the difficulties of team building in order for you to do it the right way and benefit the most from its power. It is also important to realize the fact no two companies or organizations have exactly the same needs. As such, your team building session and exercises should match your organization's unique situation.

Relative to the foregoing, to make team building sessions and exercises work for your organization, they should be able to address the root of why the members are not behaving and working as one team. The team building itself should be able to strengthen the "sense of team" in each of the employees of your organization, and this is a continuing process, not just a one-time event.

Four Team Building Difficulties to Unlock

Having said that, here are five team-building difficulties to unlock:

1. Lack of Awareness and Understanding – often, the source of conflict among members is they do not understand clearly their roles, the goals of the team, as well as the code of conduct and cooperation.

    As a result, team members usually resort to finger pointing, blaming one another, using scapegoats, and being hypercritical of one another's actions and ways. Increasing their level of awareness and understanding of their roles, goals, and implementing a code of conduct and cooperation will enable team members to de-focus on others and focus on themselves.

2. Lack of Conversational Capacity – Team issues usually escalate during critical times or when under pressure. The major cause is the lack of conversational capacity. The Weber Consulting defines this as the team's ability to engage in an open discussion without prejudices or biases.

   Teams with high conversational capacity may still disagree but their disagreements are part of resolving the issue. Teams with low conversational capacity are more likely to disagree often and over trivial matters that affect productivity and performance.

3. Misplaced Goals – while the spirit of competition may spark or stimulate enthusiasm among your employees, your team building goals should refrain from centering on competition. Instead of competition, encourage and inspire your employees to cooperate.

   While it is important to improve individual competencies, the team members should not attempt to outshine one another. They should be able to respect the identity of their team, and pull each other up to meet team goals. The interests of the team should be more valuable than self-interests.

4. Management Attitude – admit it or not, but most times, the management look at team building as the process to enable staff to change, improve, and work with one another cohesively. Management rarely, if they do, include themselves in the picture.

   The thing is that the participation of the manager or the leader is the most critical. Any organization cannot build a solid team unless the management is willing to look into its own contributions and improve as necessary.

Thanks for Previewing My Exciting Book Entitled:

"Team Building! Quickly Increase Team Building And Project Management Skills For Better Employee Engagement, Motivation, Production, And Workplace Morale!"

To purchase this book, simply go to the Amazon Kindle store and simply search:

"TEAM BUILDING"

Then just scroll down until you see my book. You will know it is mine because you will see my name "Ryan Cooper" underneath the title.

Alternatively, you can visit my author page on Amazon to see this book and other work I have done. Thanks so much, and please don't forget your free bonuses

DON'T LEAVE YET! - CHECK OUT YOUR FREE BONUSES BELOW!

Free Bonus Offer: Get Free Access To The[PotentialRise.com](PotentialRise.com) VIP Newsletter!

Once you enter your email address you will immediately get free access to this awesome newsletter!

But wait, right now if you join now for free you will also get free access to the "LIMITLESS ENERGY" free EBook!

To claim both your FREE VIP NEWSLETTER MEMBERSHIP and your FREE BONUS Ebook on LIMITLESS ENERGY!

Just Go To:

www.PotentialRise.com

www.ingramcontent.com/pod-product-compliance
Lightning Source LLC
Chambersburg PA
CBHW071549170526
45166CB00004B/1606